# 100 THINGS TO DO IN TACOMA BEFORE YOU DIE

2nd Edition

Union Station

# 100 THINGS TO DO IN TACOMA BEFORE YOU DIE

2nd Edition

PEGGY CLEVELAND

REEDY PRESS

Reedy Press
PO Box 5131
St. Louis, MO 63139, USA
reedypress.com



Library of Congress Control Number: 2025936742

ISBN: 9781681065977

Cover photo courtesy of Peggy Cleveland

Design by Jill Halpin

All photos are courtesy of the author or believed to be in the public domain unless otherwise noted.

Printed in the United States of America
25 26 27 28 29 5 4 3 2 1

# DEDICATION

To my husband, Rich,
who has encouraged my writing
dreams from the beginning.

Chihuly Bridge of Glass

# CONTENTS

**Music and Entertainment**

**Sports and Recreation**

**Shopping and Fashion**

# ACKNOWLEDGMENTS

First, I would like to acknowledge the Coast Salish People, who were the first settlers of the land that is now Tacoma and Pierce County, as well as their ancestors the Puyallup, Nisqually, Squaxin, Steilacoom, and Muckleshoot Indian Tribes. Thank you to Matt Wakefield, who helped me discover Tacoma's hidden gems. Kris Hay's input was invaluable to the Food and Drink section. Look for her upcoming cookbook *Tacoma Aroma: Savor the Flavor*. Thanks to the teams at Pretty Gritty Tours and *Grit City* magazine, who share their deep love of the history and tales of our interesting city with their tours and articles. Thanks to Adrian Milanio, a local musician, and Danno Presents, an entertainment company, for their help with the Music and Entertainment section. I'd also like to acknowledge the scrappy, small, local businesses featured in this book that make Tacoma such a special place. The community comes out in force to support online fundraising campaigns, and we now have many vibrant new businesses.

Puyallup Tribe Walk

# PREFACE

The COVID pandemic devastated Tacoma just like many areas of the country. The community strongly supported local, small businesses but alas, 10 entries in the first edition of *100 Things to Do in Tacoma Before You Die* closed. So, with sadness, I write this while also happy and hopeful for the new businesses springing up in our area. Tacoma recently received national recognition when named one of CNN Travel's "America's Best Towns to Visit in 2024," and many other accolades have followed. Tacoma no longer sits in the shadow of its more famous neighbor to the north, Seattle.

During my events for the first edition, I often received questions as to why I wrote the book since I am not from the area. I counter with, I am the perfect person to write this book because I have insider knowledge of a local with the fresh perspective of someone new to the area. The proof is when locals share with me, "I never knew this was in Tacoma."

Tacoma continues to shine with access to Mount Rainier National Park, a vibrant downtown with both museum and theater districts, and waterfront activities in Commencement Bay and the Puget Sound. This book includes 100 things to do but not all are in downtown Tacoma. Visitors and locals alike will enjoy exploring the Greater Tacoma area and Pierce County.

Three Hearts Tacoma

# FOOD AND DRINK

1

# BE STUNNED
## BY THE VIEWS AT COPPER & SALT NORTHWEST KITCHEN

Prepare to be stunned by the gorgeous views from the dining room at Copper & Salt Northwest Kitchen. Breathtaking views of Commencement Bay and the Olympic Mountains from the floor-to-ceiling windows add to the ambience, and you might even see an orca breach the water from your table. How cool is that! Sip a craft cocktail infused with the freshest of local ingredients before indulging in artisan dishes that capture the spirit of the Northwest. This is real food sourced from local farmers and makers, then creatively prepared for a very memorable meal. Make sure to try the burrata starter, which takes fresh creamy cheese and garnishes it with seasonal fruits or vegetables. So simple and so tasty.

5125 Grand Loop, Ruston, 253-319-8290
copperandsaltnw.com

**TIP**

When finished dining, check out the hotel's gift shop, which offers a variety of local and regional products for sale.

# JOIN YOUR NEIGHBORS
## AT COOKS TAVERN

Located in the heart of the Proctor District, Cooks Tavern is a neighborhood staple. It is the perfect incarnation for a building that has always housed community businesses. Walking into the building, visitors find themselves in a cozy destination that has the feel of a beloved tavern with dark wood and brick accents. The menu is eclectic with strong New Orleans influences with a Pacific Northwest twist. Enjoy breakfast, lunch, or dinner with breakfast served until 3 p.m. The fresh beignets served warm in a paper bag shaken with powder sugar are a popular item. On Sundays enjoy the Sunday Night Family Style Chicken Supper, and Thursday evenings also offer a special meal. No tavern is complete without signature cocktails, and Cooks pours some great brunch-themed ones with and without the booze. Wine lovers will enjoy the brown bag special for a set price for a bottle of white or red; the choice a surprise.

3201 N 26th St., 253-327-1777
cookstavern.com

3

# NOSH ON FRESH BAGELS
## AT HOWDY BAGEL

Jake Carter and his partner, Daniel Blagovich, took Tacoma by storm with their delectable bagels when they opened their shop in May 2023. The kitschy cowboy decor adds a fun vibe. Their yummy bagels have a crisp, shiny crust with a soft, chewy inside. Pair with a whipped schmear (a flavored cream cheese) or order as a tasty breakfast sandwich. All menu items are cooked to order and prepared with fresh, local ingredients. Guests can personalize a bagel sandwich with 16 different add-ons including spicy tomato jam, Howdy Sauce, and a local berry jam. Prepare to wait. Even on weekdays you'll find a line out the door.

Sadly, Carter was murdered on January 5, 2024, while on vacation in New Orleans with Blagovich. The event shocked the local community, who rallied to raise $303,125 to support the Howdy Bagel family as they navigated this tragedy. In just two short years, Howdy Bagel has become a beloved fixture of the Tacoma culinary scene.

5421 S Tacoma Way, 253-301-1586
howdybagel.com

### TIP

Howdy Bagel is wildly popular with lines out the door, so plan to visit on a weekday. There will still be a line, just not as long.

4

# SUPPORT THE ENVIRONMENT
## AT TABLE 47

Located in an upscale bowling alley and laser tag venue, Table 47 is a pleasant surprise. This farm-to-table restaurant takes reducing their environmental footprint to a whole new level. From the busy worm farm in the basement composting scraps to the geothermal heating and cooling, this is a business that is passionate about the environment. Planet-friendly food is sourced from local farmers who share the same values, while microgreens are grown right in the restaurant. What this means for you is a fresh, flavorful meal. Simple comfort foods such as flatbreads and burgers become a gourmet treat when prepared with fresh, local ingredients. Craft cocktails, local beer, and a simple but well-thought-out wine list enhance the meal. Once you are full, head into Ocean5 to work off the calories with bowling or a game of laser tag.

5268 Point Fosdick Dr., 253-857-4777
t47.com

5

# GET NOSTALGIC
## AT BEN DEW'S CLUBHOUSE GRILL & COCKTAIL BAR

This Tacoma institution opened in 1954 as Ben Dew's Patio Café. After a closure in the '80s, the new owners brought the business back as Ben Dew's Clubhouse Grill & Cocktail Bar. It still has its original historic charm. A big stone fireplace dominates the dark interior while wagon wheel chandeliers bring light to the high wood ceiling. It's the type of place with huge breakfasts and Sunday dinners. When you are nostalgic for old-fashioned comfort food, Ben Dew's fits the bill. The Sunday Night Family Dinner sells from 2 p.m. until it's gone and includes their famous fried chicken. The extensive menu includes a classic favorites section with chicken and dumplings, homemade meat loaf, and eight more timeless entrées. Watch a game at the cocktail bar and try the Signature Clubhouse Mary made with a special house Bloody Mary mix.

6501 6th Ave., 253-564-4442
bendewsclubhouse.getbento.com

## TIP

The house-made refrigerator jam is so popular that guests can now purchase take-home containers of it.

6

# DEVOUR A DOUGHNUT

## AT LEGENDARY DOUGHNUTS

So yummy! These doughnuts really are legendary and the most creative you will find anywhere. Can doughnuts be art? These handcrafted creations sure are. The most popular is the Oprah bar, a raised bar doughnut frosted with maple and topped with freshly cooked bacon. Legendary is also known for its innovation "the doughsant," which is a croissant–doughnut fusion that is more of a dessert than a breakfast treat. There are 30 to 35 treats in the case each day, made fresh daily from premium ingredients. The selection includes those named after famous people and inspired by candy bars such as the Almond Joy and the Snickers bar. Adults will love the boozy balls, which are raised, glazed ball-shape doughnuts filled with BSB (local Heritage Distilling's Brown Sugar Bourbon) or Bailey's Cream. If sweet is not your thing, try a grilled doughnut panini, a "doughnut bun" filled with savory meats and cheeses.

2602 6th Ave., 253-327-1327
legendarydoughnuts.com

7

# EXPLORE THIS ASIAN MARKET
## AND TRY SOMETHING NEW AT PAL DO WORLD

Locals in the know head to the last restaurant in the Pal Do World food court, the House of Mandoo, which serves only one thing: freshly made mandoo. These fist-sized dumplings are generously filled with spicy pork, regular pork, or bean curd. The dough is light and fluffy, and you can often see it being handmade, then filled and steamed to perfection. This gastronomic delight is a perfect starter while you wait for your meal from the other vendors. Pair your mandoo with Chinese, Japanese, or Korean meals from other restaurants in the food court. Most are served with fresh banchan, which are traditional side dishes such as kimchi. After your meal, explore the market, which includes a bakery, ginseng retail shop, and a Korean grocery store that has tanks for fresh seafood.

9701 S Tacoma Way, Lakewood, 253-267-0609
facebook.com/houseofmandoo

8

# TRY A HEALTHY BISON BURGER
## AT TATANKA TAKE-OUT

Tatanka Take-Out delights with its delicious menu of American comfort foods and burgers prepared with bison meat. Owner Nathan Thomas started out as a longtime customer and then became an employee when the original owner needed help. He never thought about owning a restaurant, but the opportunity to own an established business with a product he could stand behind was too good to pass up.

Bison is America's original health food. It is a nutrient-dense meat packed full of essential fatty acids and protein. Also known as buffalo, these animals roam freely and subsist on grass and hay. No antibiotics or growth hormones are ever used. Thomas is a one-man show and a font of knowledge when it comes to bison. The menu offers a variety of burgers, burritos, and tacos with creative side dishes. Vegetarian options are also available. While you wait, check out all the bison artwork and memorabilia.

4915 N Pearl St., Ruston, 253-752-8778
tatanka-to.com

## TIP

Thomas also makes a killer bison lasagna. Pick up a pan from the freezer to take home and bake.

9

# BRUNCH
## AT THREE HEARTS TACOMA

Three Hearts Tacoma brings people together at the Hilltop location. The Hellis and Eder families created the café with a passion for community, food, and coffee. The space is bright and dominated by a mural of an octopus with three hearts hidden in its tentacles. The octopus is Tacoma's mascot, and young Wyatt Hellis learned in school about how they have three hearts. This story inspired the name of the restaurant and epitomizes the owners' love poured into this business.

The moment you walk through the door, the scents of fresh bakery goods and coffee make this place feel like home. The menu is filled with nostalgic foods such as the classic Dutch Baby. This skillet puffy pancake is a delectable treat, or order the savory version for a hearty breakfast. For those with dietary restrictions, there are lots of options and no extra charge for gluten-free.

1116 M.L.K. Jr. Way, 253-201-7742
threeheartstacoma.com

### TIP

Unlike most bakeries, Three Hearts has a large selection of savory pastries such as a pulled pork croissant and a brioche of bacon, egg, and cheese. Make sure to try them.

# CHOMP DOWN
## ON A GOURMET HOT DOG AT THE RED HOT

This Tacoma institution is in the vibrant Sixth Avenue District, a hip area of local restaurants, bars, and shops. The creative geniuses working the kitchen have elevated the lowly hot dog to a whole new level of dining sophistication. The extensive menu includes an amazing selection of hot dogs, sausages, and even vegan fare. You can order a classic or try something new. The "Whole Lotta Rosie" loads a bun up with rosemary-chicken sausage, rémoulade, white cheddar, grilled onions, and arugula. So unique. Every Thursday, the Red Hot rolls out a new or seasonal creation so there is always something new to try. Desserts consist of old-time favorites like the MoonPie and Cracker Jack. This is an over-21 establishment with a great selection of Pacific Northwest craft beer on tap. If you have little ones, takeout is available.

2914 6th Ave., 253-779-0229
redhottacoma.com

11

# DISCOVER
## BUDDY'S CHICKEN & WAFFLES

It is so appropriate that when Uncle Thurms Soul Food, a renowned Black-owned business in the historic Lincoln District, closed, Buddy's Chicken & Waffles took over the space. Buddy Brown's crispy fried chicken and unique waffles have a cult following in Tacoma. The community stepped up to support his fundraising efforts to open a restaurant. His social media posts detailing his interaction with the city during the permitting process are legendary.

With all the hurdles in the past, Buddy's serves up some seriously good chicken. He marinates it overnight in his secret blend then hand breads the chicken for a crispy crunch on the outside and juicy flavor on the inside. Select from a variety of waffles that change seasonally. The flavors are creative, such as Cinnamon Toast Crunch or cookies and cream. Select from a variety of unique syrups. Hot honey bourbon maple syrup is a local favorite.

3709 S G St., 253-201-1550
instagram.com/buddyschickenandwaffles

# TAKE IN WATERFRONT VIEWS

## AT NETSHED NO. 9

In the early 1900s, Gig Harbor bustled with a vibrant fishing industry. At the end of the day, fishermen returning home would count the net sheds. More than 100 years later, these old buildings house local businesses. Number 9 no longer has musty nets but instead fills with the smell of fresh cinnamon rolls each morning.

NetShed No. 9 is known for its breakfast. Order a skillet of warm cinnamon rolls for the table. Guests can choose the O.G. Roll (a classic roll) or go for the Uncommon Roll, which changes every day. The restaurant uses 100-year-old cast iron waffle makers, which create a crisp waffle. For an indulgent treat try the P.B. & J. Waffle, a light and fluffy waffle slathered with creamy peanut butter, drizzled with raspberry syrup, topped with fresh raspberries and roasted peanuts, then pipped with fresh whipped Chantilly. Yummy!

3313 Harborview Dr., Gig Harbor, 253-858-7175
netshed9.com

13

# SCREAM FOR ICE CREAM
## AT ICE CREAM SOCIAL

Ice Cream Social takes this simple dessert to a whole new level of yumminess. You can smell the freshly baking waffle cones well before you enter the shop. Layla Isaac created Ice Cream Social because she wanted to make something that would bring a smile to people's faces, and everybody loves ice cream. She is a self-taught ice cream maker who crafts her unique flavors from natural, local ingredients. Ice Cream Social has a loyal following due to its great-tasting product. Quality ingredients really make a difference. There are three shops in Tacoma, but the one located at Point Ruston will give you the best experience. There is nothing like ordering a crispy waffle cone filled with your favorite flavors and taking it out to the waterfront to stroll while enjoying this delectable treat. There are also plenty of benches with scenic views for miles.

## LOCATIONS

**Ruston**

5107 Main St., 253-507-5448

**Proctor**

2521 N Proctor St., 253-327-1803

**Hilltop**

1110 M.L.K. Jr. Way, 253-327-1660

icecreamsocialtacoma.com

# DIG INTO TASTY BURGERS
## AT THE ICONIC FRISKO FREEZE

The retro style of this 1950s iconic landmark will take you back in time. It is Tacoma's most renowned burger joint. It is still owned by descendants of the original owner. You'll find everyone from moms in fancy cars to high schoolers in pickup trucks eating here. Drive up or head to the walk-up window to order from the simple menu of burgers, fries, and shakes. The burgers are hot, juicy messes with a secret sauce, pickles, onions, ketchup, and lettuce all wrapped up in a wax bag. These are thin patties that cook quickly with a subtle crispness, so make sure to order a double. Get plenty of napkins, because the only dining space is in your car. On busy Saturday nights this place is hopping, and you may have to wait a bit, but the burgers are so worth the wait.

1201 Division Ave., 253-272-6843
friskofreeze.com

## MORE GREAT TACOMA BURGERS

**Shake Shake Shake**

124 N Tacoma Ave.
253-507-4060
missionpoint.com

**Patty's Burgers**

5615 S Tacoma Way
253-474-0844

**Lefty's Burger Shack**

8317 27th St. W, University Place
253-565-0887

# GET BOMBED
## AT TIBBITTS@FERNHILL

Get bombed, not on alcohol but on food. It's rare to find a unique dish for the breakfast game but Chef Shawn Tibbitts has done it with his lobster bomb. It is one of the most unusual but tasty breakfast creations you will ever eat. He starts with a toasted bread bowl, then loads it up with champagne-soaked lobster, candied bacon, Yukon gold potatoes, sherry fennel, scrambled eggs, avocado, and farm-fresh greens, all smothered in a lemony hollandaise sauce. What makes it so amazing is he cooks it all on camp stove–type burners in a teeny, tiny kitchen. The restaurant is very small, with just a few tables, so reservations are a must. Tibbitts@FernHill has a big heart, and it shows through the love he puts into preparing each dish. His friendly touch comes across as he takes time to visit tables and greet his guests.

8237 S Park Ave., 253-327-1334
tibbittsfernhillreservation.com

### TIP

After dining, walk next door to look at the murals. Fern Hill is a Tacoma Historic Neighborhood Business District.

# EXPLORE NEW TASTES
## AT NEW GANGNAM BBQ

If you aren't familiar with Korean food and culture, do yourself a favor and try Korean barbeque. The New Gangnam BBQ is in the heart of the Lakewood International district also known as Korea Town. The restaurant serves Korean-style barbecue that you cook at your table, which is equipped with a gas grill. You can order from the menu or just go with the all-you-can-eat option. Order the types of meat you wish to cook from the list and then, next thing you know, a server will roll a cart over and begin placing a variety of banchan (Korean side dishes), a bowl of cooked rice, soy sauce, and a bean paste on your table. Make sure to order the bulgogi, which is a marinated beef that is so tasty. Cook the meat over the grill and then eat separately or take a lettuce leaf, fill it with rice, meat, and pickled vegetable from the banchan, and top it with bean paste before eating it like a taco. Most of the patrons are Korean, which says a lot about the authenticity of the restaurant.

9104 S Tacoma Way, Lakewood, 253-581-1200
newgangnam.com

17

# CROSS THE CHIHULY BRIDGE OF GLASS TO EAT
## IN INDITA MIA

Just a short stroll from downtown Tacoma via the Chihuly Bridge of Glass, Indita Mia's scratch-made Mexican food shines in its new location. It's tucked in below the Thea's Landing Waterfront Apartments and adjacent to the Museum of Glass. Gorgeous floor-to-ceiling windows overlook Thea Foss Waterway, and on a sunny day guests may catch a glimpse of Mount Rainier. The interior impresses with a 900-pound madrone tree trunk imported from Mexico that dominates the bar area.

Owners Angie and Oreb Apodaca's family recipes shine when premium fresh ingredients are incorporated into the dishes. The two want to share authentic Mexican cuisine with Tacoma. Their carne asada is made from thinly sliced prime rib eye, which enhances the quality of this dish. Try the chicharrón de queso, a crispy cheese tortilla filled with Wagyu shredded beef and topped with cilantro, pickled onions, and a drizzle of cilantro crema.

1715 Dock St., 253-301-1784
inditamia.restaurant

## TIP

After lunch, take a walk along the Thea Foss Public Esplanade, a three-mile trail.

18

# PACK A PICNIC
## FROM THE METROPOLITAN MARKET

The Metropolitan Market is a chain of upscale markets that will delight foodies with premium ingredients and local products. With so many great options for both hot and cold takeout, it is no wonder so many visit just for a meal. According to the *Seattle Times* food writer Tan Vinh, "The Met Market prime rib is arguably the most underrated sandwich in Seattle." You can second that for Tacoma. The all-day tradition of flame-roasting prime rib to perfection began 20 years ago. Thinly sliced and piled high on a crispy, fresh baguette topped with horseradish sauce and served with au jus for dipping. Divine! For dessert you can't miss the "Cookie." This delectable mass of a chocolate chip cookie oozes warm Belgian chocolate, both semisweet and bittersweet Callebaut, from its buttery goodness. Baked fresh all day and placed on warming stones, you can enjoy this treat like it just came out of the oven all day. The perfect ending to a gourmet, grocery store meal. Grab picnic fixings and head to Point Defiance Park for an alfresco meal.

### TIP

If you prefer to eat at the Met, it has a heated outdoor patio with seating. Then you can explore the shops in the Proctor District.

19

# EAT A HEARTY BREAKFAST

## AT THE HOMESTEAD RESTAURANT & BAKERY

This is not your fancy, hoity-toity brunch spot but rather where people go for a big, stick-to-your-ribs breakfast. You can't miss the big, red barn that houses the family-owned Homestead Restaurant & Bakery, which has dished up ginormous breakfasts for over 30 years. The focus is comfort food from recipes and ingredients that reflect the family's heritage. The vintage Western theme is fun, and tables have screens that scroll through photos of menu items. It is so hard to decide, so here are a few suggestions to narrow down your choices. They are famed for serving chicken-fried steak nine different ways. One of the more infamous ways is the "Squatch," as in "Bigfoot." Homemade fry bread is slathered with Alfredo sauce, then topped with three eggs scrambled with bell peppers, onions, mushrooms, a half-pound chicken-fried steak, and more Alfredo sauce. With cinnamon rolls the size of your head, the "Wagon Wheel" is more than enough to share. The Homestead's renowned cinnamon rolls are sliced and made into French toast, which is then stuffed with ham, bacon, crispy hash browns, and American cheese, then drizzled with icing.

7837 S Tacoma Way, 253-476-9000
homesteadwa.com

## TIP

After your meal, take a drive on South Tacoma Way to look at all the cars. The road is lined on both sides with auto dealers, and some have classic car collections.

# INDULGE IN PACIFIC ISLAND CUISINE

## AT WOVEN

Woven took the Tacoma food scene by storm when it opened in 2024. The Puyallup Tribe purchased the property overlooking Commencement Bay and the Puget Sound, bringing ancestral lands back under their stewardship. In partnership with Pacific Northwest Chef Roy Yamaguchi, they founded Woven, a restaurant dedicated to weaving the flavors of Hawaii, Asia, and the Pacific Northwest together. Reservations are a must. Walking in the front door, guests' senses are teased with the scent of a cherrywood fire, the sounds of sizzling pans, and the stunning waterfront views. The Misoyaki glazed black cod is a staff favorite as are the beef short ribs, so tender they melt in your mouth. Fresh local ingredients and the fusion of cultures make this a menu like no other.

3017 Ruston Way, 253-650-9500
eatwoven.com

### TIP

Seasonally, take a scenic flight over the Puget Sound. Kenmore Air's partnership with the Puyallup Tribe offers flights from the same building as Woven. If you want to step up your romance game, schedule a flight followed by a delectable dinner at Woven.

## OTHER RUSTON WAY RESTAURANTS

**Duke's Seafood**

3327 Ruston Way, 253-752-5444
dukesseafood.com

**Lobster Shop**

4015 Ruston Way, 253-759-2165
lobstershop.com

**Katie Downs Waterfront Tavern**

3211 Ruston Way, 253-756-0771
katiedowns.com

Tacoma Glass Gallery and Fusion Studio

# MUSIC AND ENTERTAINMENT

# BE SERENADED
## ON THE GIG HARBOR GONDOLA

This is not your average harbor cruise. Climb aboard an authentic Venetian gondola named *Nelly* after the original owner's mother. John Synco, the gondolier and owner, shares tales of Gig Harbor history and serenades guests as he propels the boat through the water utilizing Venetian rowing, a style that uses just one oar. The harbor is scenic rain or shine, but a clear day provides stunning views of Mount Rainier and the tiny Gig Harbor Lighthouse. The gondola is surprisingly spacious and can carry six passengers. It is truly a unique way to explore this lovely body of water. You can preorder an appetizer box or bring your own food and drinks. I suggest your favorite bottle of Washington State wine. Truly a unique experience.

Meet at the Gig Harbor Marina
3117 Harborview Dr., Gig Harbor, 253-432-0052
gigharborgondola.com

# STEP ONTO THE GREENS
## AT TOWER LANES ENTERTAINMENT CENTER

When the rain gets you down, head to Tower Lanes Entertainment Center's mini golf course to chase away the blues. The 18-hole lighted course meanders past waterfalls, bridges, and fountains. The setting may be peaceful, but this is one challenging course. Adults can check out the 19th Hole for their favorite libations.

Traditional bowling lanes are fun, but for something new try Glow Bowling. Dancing lights, top music hits, and glowing bowling balls bring added fun. For those who want to take their bowling to the next level, check out the Super 8 Pro Shop for advice on equipment. The arcade is a huge room with games and multiple pool tables. The restaurant is very popular with families for breakfast. The menu is huge with all the traditional breakfast favorites such as omelets, chicken-fried steak, and pancakes. It opens early before the attractions so enjoy a hearty meal before bowling or mini golf.

6323 6th Ave., 253-564-8853
towerlanes.net

23

# CHILL OUT TO LIVE MUSIC
## AT THE SPANISH BALLROOM

The Spanish Bar and Ballroom at McMenamins Elks Temple is the place to be for live music in Tacoma. A variety of genres are offered in this grand space, typically from Wednesday through Sunday each week. Built in 1916, the Elks Temple was once the site of ballroom dancing and other events. The building is on the National Register of Historic Places and is now reimagined as a vibrant gathering place. With grand chandeliers and ornate trim, the Spanish Ballroom can hold 700, which is enough of a crowd for high energy but still intimate in size. Check out the upstairs bar, which overlooks the ballroom for an elevated view of the stage. The live music concerts feature some of the top bands in the country with a fantastic, diverse schedule. Country, rock, pop, and even acoustic guitar artists appear on the monthly schedules. Most nights the music is free, but check the schedule for ticketed concerts.

565 Broadway, 253-300-8754
mcmenamins.com/elks-temple/spanish-ballroom

## TIP

Make sure to check out the Spanish Steps, which are adjacent to McMenamins Elks Temple. The steps, constructed in 1916 to connect Broadway and Commerce Street, were modeled after the more famous Scalinata di Spagna (Spanish Steps) in Rome. The City of Tacoma recognized the historical importance and restored the steps in 2011.

# DRIVE A FORD MODEL T
## AT THE LEMAY COLLECTIONS AT MARYMOUNT

Fans of the Fox Business series *Strange Inheritance* will be familiar with Harold LeMay's collection of more than 3,000 cars. It was listed in the *Guinness Book of World Records 1997* as the largest privately owned car collection in the world. You truly experience the sheer immensity of this collection when you tour the family's museum, which contains the bulk of the collection. If you time it right, you can book a "Model T Experience" and learn the history of this famous car and how Henry Ford's "Tin Lizzie" made car ownership available to the masses. The car has three foot pedals, one hand lever, and two hand controls, making it a challenge to drive. You will receive instruction, and once you have the hang of it you can drive around the historic Marymount Academy campus with its beautiful Douglas fir forest.

325 152nd St. E, 253-272-2336
lemaymarymount.org

## TIP

Make sure to tour the grounds during your visit and explore the Rodin Sculpture Garden, which features some of Rodin's famous works, like *The Thinker*, cast from the original molds.

# TAKE IN A MOVIE
## AT THE BLUE MOUSE THEATRE

Located in the historic Proctor District, the Blue Mouse Theatre is the oldest continuously operating theater in Washington state. Since 1923, and through many owners, it has become a treasured community space. Each month, guests can enjoy first-run movies as well as classic favorites like *The Rocky Horror Picture Show*. Check the calendar for concerts and live events. During the COVID-19 pandemic, venue upgrades were completed.

The theater has a fascinating history that intersects with famed native son Dale Chihuly. During renovations, he is rumored to have helped uncover a neon tube in the venue's marquee. It inspired him to design the iconic blue neon mice that appear to scamper around the marquee and clocks at night. Guests can enjoy freshly popped Blue Mouse popcorn, their favorite candy, and local beer and wines at the concession stand.

2611 N Proctor St., 253-752-9500
bluemousetheatre.com

**TIP**

Before or after a movie enjoy one of the many restaurants or bars in the Proctor District, all within walking distance of the theater.

26

# DISCOVER THE DARK SIDE OF TIKI
## AT DEVIL'S REEF

Tiki is a Polynesian symbol with a variety of meanings and cultural significance. Owners Jason Alexander and Robyn Murphy have given tiki decor, symbolism, and even tiki mugs a unique spin at their bar Devil's Reef. The venue is so dark that even after your eyes adjust to the dim light it is still dark. Shelves behind the bar house exotic rum bottles and Jason's tiki mug collection. The decor could be described as a blending of Disney's Pirates of the Caribbean ride with the haunted house.

Recent drinks on the menu have frightening names like "The Yawn of the Dark Universe Belching Forth Aimless Black Planets of Unknown Horror." Tiki bars have cult followings, and Devil's Reef is no exception. Guests have visited from all over the world. The cocktail menu is extensive and rum heavy. Light bites are available along with fancy dessert specials.

706 Ct. C, 253-983-7850
devils-reef.wa-cafe.com

# GET SERIOUS ABOUT GAMING

## AT OCEAN5

Ocean5 is an upscale entertainment complex that takes family-friendly fun to a whole new level. Adults will love it, too. Walking through the door into the immense lobby, you will be enthralled with the huge hanging art that resembles fish scales. There is a giant 360-degree fireplace with circular seating around it that is the perfect spot to enjoy a latte or a craft cocktail. Activities include 22 lanes of bowling with classic 10-pin or duckpin. You can even reserve a suite. The laser arena is two stories tall and can have up to 40 players per game. The modern arcade has classic favorites as well as the latest in game machines. Earn points to redeem for fabulous prizes. The latest addition to Ocean5 is the Top Golf Swing Suites. This virtual experience allows you to play your favorite golf courses. Adults will love the fully stocked bar with the best of Pacific Northwest distillers, brewers, and winemakers.

5268 Point Fosdick Dr., Gig Harbor, 253-857-7529
o5social.com

28

# ROCK OUT
## AT THE TACOMA DOME

The Tacoma Dome is the venue that hosts big crowd events. It is one of the largest wood-domed structures in the world. With the recent addition of telescopic seating, the dome hosts events for up to 21,000. Many a graduate from one of Tacoma's high schools has walked across a stage here to receive their diploma. This is the place to see big-name concerts and other world-class entertainment like monster trucks. Annual events include the Tacoma RV Show and the Tacoma Home and Garden Show. The venue has plenty of parking. If you have some time to spare, LeMay - America's Car Museum is adjacent to the Tacoma Dome and showcases a variety of automobiles, including some from the Harold LeMay Collection. The Tacoma Dome Station is the terminus for the Tacoma Link light-rail, which provides an easy way to explore downtown.

2727 E D St., 253-272-3663
tacomadome.org

# WATCH A VARIETY OF EVENTS AT THE EMERALD QUEEN EVENT CENTER

Driving I-5 in Tacoma, you can't miss the grand Emerald Queen Casino with its flashing lights and billboards. The artwork and architectural features were designed by Puyallup tribal members and feature traditional and contemporary symbols of the Coast Salish. The artwork is on a scale such that you can see it from the interstate. The state-of-the-art Emerald Queen Event Center is Tacoma's newest venue for live music and has stadium seating for 1,800-plus. With luxurious theater-style seating and immersive audio, it takes concertgoing to a whole new level. Look for national concert tours, MMA fights, and other events throughout the year. Check out the casino after your concert. The $400 million property features Vegas-style gaming and has more than 2,100 slots, 60 table games, and six dining venues. There is also a brand-new hotel on-site.

5700 Pacific Hwy. E, Fife, 253-594-7777
emeraldqueen.com/tickets

# TAKE IN A SHOW
## AT TACOMA'S THEATER DISTRICT

The Tacoma Theater District is a vibrant area of the city offering world-class artists performing year-round. There is really something for everyone. The district consists of three theaters that host eight resident arts organizations. Offerings include special events, Broadway shows, ballets, symphonies, live comedy, concerts in a variety of genres, and musicals. The Pantages Theater dates to 1918 and is one of the oldest Pantages Theaters still in operation. The Rialto Theater is also historic and opened in 1918. It was originally a movie house with beautiful Beaux-Arts features that still exist today. The Theatre on the Square is the newest of the three, opening in 1993. Plan a night at the theater; there are many local restaurants close by for a meal or post-show cocktails.

The Pantages Theater
901 Broadway

The Rialto Theater
310 S 9th St.

The Theatre on the Square
915 Broadway

253-591-5890
tacomacitytheaters.org

# TAKE A PRETTY GRITTY TOUR

When the owners of the company are veteran travelers who have been on their fair share of boring tours, you know they will have a higher standard. Chris Staudinger and Tawny Clark have raised the bar when it comes to providing a variety of fun and interesting tours of Tacoma. History, food, or drink tours abound, and if you don't see something you like, book a custom tour. A "Get to Know Tacoma" tour gives a great introduction to the gritty city, but there is so much more.

The "Late Night Stadium High Tour" explores Stadium High School, famed for its impressive French Château architecture. The movie *10 Things I Hate About You* was filmed at the school, adding to its fame. Coffee and beer are beverages of choice in Tacoma, and there is a tour for each. For those who love the iconic candy Almond Roca, made by Brown and Haley in Tacoma, the "Sweets Tour" is for you. Learn all about the history of Tacoma's tasty treats.

253-242-4715, prettygrittytours.com

# LEARN TO FUSE GLASS
## AT THE TACOMA GLASS GALLERY AND FUSING STUDIO

Get your creative juices flowing with a glass fusing experience at the Tacoma Glass Gallery and Fusing Studio. Layers of glass melt together in a kiln to create unique works of art. Guests design and assemble their pieces, starting with a clear, flat tile, and can work at their own pace for up to two hours. Pricing includes all supplies, instruction, and tools with add-ons available for an additional price.

The studio has plenty of examples for inspiration. Start with a flat tile, add bits of colored glass to create a design, and layer it onto the tile. It takes more than 15 hours in the kiln to fuse the project. Guests can pick up their artwork in one week. The studio also has a beautiful gift shop with stunning pieces of blown or fused glass for purchase. If glass blowing is more your style, visit their downtown Tacoma location.

Tacoma Glass Gallery & Fusing Studio
2621 N Proctor St., Ste. B

Tacoma Glassblowing Studio
114 S 23rd St.

253-383-3499
tacomaglassblowing.com

# DIVE INTO THIS DIVE BAR
## AT BOB'S JAVA JIVE

This iconic coffeepot-shaped building built in 1927 is home to Bob's Java Jive, a Tacoma landmark that gives new meaning to the term "dive bar." When the COVID-19 pandemic took its toll, people from around the world contributed money and labor to save this much-beloved coffeepot on the National Register of Historic Places. Enjoy karaoke most nights with some seriously good locals belting out tunes. Before their success, the Ventures, famed for the song "Wipe Out," were the house band. Rumor has it, Nirvana either played here or was rejected to play here—that is the great thing about a legendary venue: the stories and rumors. The interior still has remnants of the tiki hut decor popular in the 1950s, although the jungle vines are gone due to the fire code, as are the monkeys Java and Jive.

2102 S Tacoma Way, 253-475-9843
facebook.com/bobsjavajive

# PARTY
## AT JAZZBONES

When you ask a local where to see live music, Jazzbones is sure to come up in the conversation. Located in the popular Sixth Avenue District, Jazzbones will delight live-music lovers. Check their calendar for upcoming events. You'll find local, regional, and national artists performing a variety of musical styles; themed music nights; and even rockaroke, which is karaoke performed with a live band. How cool is that! Jazzbones is also a nightclub with the hottest DJs and a restaurant with a surprisingly eclectic menu, offering up bar food as well as vegan options such as a cauliflower filet. There is even a mojito-themed pizza. For those who want their own space, book the private balcony, which offers great views of the band or DJ performing.

2803 6th Ave., 253-396-9169
jazzbones.com

# FIND YOUR INNER LUMBERJACK

## AT THE AXE ACADEMY

Forged axe throwing has become very popular in the Pacific Northwest. It is a deceptively simple activity where you fling an axe with all your might at a target. The challenge is to get the axe to stick in the target so you can score. The Axe Academy has trained and certified coaches who take the time to demonstrate the proper throwing technique while taking you through a few practice runs. Then there are fun games to play on digitally projected targets, each one unique. Lanes will hold up to six people, and children 8 and above are welcome. A very fun change of pace instead of bowling. The Axe Academy offers prepackaged food and nonalcoholic beverages, but you are welcome to bring in food from a nearby restaurant.

705 Court C, #307, 253-350-2526
axeacademy.net

# FIND A TREASURE
## AT HI-VOLTAGE RECORDS AND BOOKS

A visit to Hi-Voltage Records and Books offers more than just shopping; it is an entertainment experience. Vinyl aficionados will love that this shop is owned and operated by musicians. Customer service has a depth of music knowledge that is what makes a local record shop so great. Each week, find the latest in new vinyl releases or browse through the used vinyl and CD collection. This store has a massive collection of over 40,000 records and CDs. Everything is graded and well organized, so it is easy to find what you are looking for. Take advantage of the music knowledge and ask for a recommendation so you can enjoy a new find. Hi-Voltage recently added books to their offerings, which expands the appeal. Merchandise includes band T-shirts as well as their own label items, which utilize their cool Hi-Voltage logo.

2714 6th Ave., 253-627-4278
hivoltagerecords.com

### TIP

Take some time to explore the 6th Avenue neighborhood, which has one of the highest concentrations of stores, restaurants, bars, and coffee shops in Tacoma.

# SING ALONG
## WITH DUELING MUSICIANS AT KEYS ON MAIN

Get ready for an energetic good time with the Dueling Piano Show at Keys on Main. Talented musicians duke it out on two grand pianos on the main stage. The show is interactive, and you can throw out a request, but it will cost you $20 to get it played. Pretty much anything played on the radio in the last 65 years is game. The piano players know thousands of songs from all genres of music. See if you can stump them with a song they don't know. It is a very rowdy atmosphere encouraged by the musicians. Full bar but no food. You can order takeout to be delivered to your table or bring in your own food. Keys on Main is very popular, especially on weekends. Make sure to secure a reservation so you are not disappointed. This is an over-21 establishment, and the banter between pianists and the audience can get racy at times.

1003 Pacific Ave., 253-627-7555
keysonmain.com/tacoma-homepage

# LAUGH OUT LOUD
## AT THE TACOMA COMEDY CLUB

Enjoy a night out at the Tacoma Comedy Club with a rotating roster of regional and national touring comedians performing on the weekends. Prices are surprisingly affordable to see comedians you'll recognize from television. Have you ever wanted to try your hand at comedy? Check out New Talent Tuesdays and Open Mic Wednesdays. Admission is free these two nights, and you may discover the next Jerry Seinfeld or watch the worst comic ever, but, hey, it's free. This lively club also offers a full food and drink menu. Seating is cabaret style with small tables that seat four to six. Make a reservation to book the best seats and pay the lowest price on tickets. Same-day tickets are available at the door if any spots remain available.

933 Market St., 253-282-7203
tacomacomedyclub.com

# PLAY SOME GAMES
## AT DORKY'S ARCADE

Dorky's Arcade in downtown Tacoma is an insanely popular 1980s-style arcade with all your favorite vintage arcade games, including Donkey Kong and Defender. The interior has an industrial feel with bare brick walls adorned with graffiti murals. It is gritty, just like Tacoma. Dorky's just passed their 20th anniversary and has developed quite a following among game enthusiasts. Reviews can be found on YouTube from visitors as far away as Japan. The arcade was also featured in a national T-Mobile commercial, the proceeds from which helped make improvements to this small business. In addition to arcade games, you'll find a huge selection of vintage pinball machines, including the Addams Family, which is the bestselling pinball machine of all time. After 9 p.m. the arcade turns into a bar with plenty of beer and an over-21 crowd. The DJ booth has a killer sound system to rock out to while trying to match your '80s scores on your favorite game.

754 Pacific Ave., 253-627-4156
dorkysarcade.com

# ENJOY COMMUNITY THEATER AT THE TACOMA MUSICAL PLAYHOUSE

The Tacoma Musical Playhouse's (TMP) mission is "Inspiring and enriching lives of our diverse community through musical theater." Since its inception in 1994, founder Jon Douglas Rake has strived to share the uniquely American art form of musical theater. Each season the theater company produces six musicals including many classic favorites. The theater company also produces a few TMP Family Theater productions each season.

For each production, the company offers a "Go Behind the Curtain" experience that takes place the week before the opening of a new production. The informative preview is perfect for families to help educate children on the theater experience. Guests get insight into the costumes, makeup, the set, and how the rehearsal pulls it all together. The TMP also has a robust education department that hosts a theater camp, acting and dance classes, and workshops. There is even a "Young at Heart" program for older performers.

7116 6th Ave., 253-565-6867
tmp.org

View of Mt. Rainier

# SPORTS AND RECREATION

# TAKE ME OUT TO THE BALL GAME
## WITH THE TACOMA RAINIERS

There is nothing like a sunny, summer day to enjoy a baseball game. Head over to Cheney Stadium to cheer on the Tacoma Rainiers, a Triple-A affiliate of the Seattle Mariners and a member of the Triple-A West. Cheney Stadium has hosted teams since 1960. Renovations in 2010 created a state-of-the-art entertainment venue where you can watch a game from stadium seats or a luxury suite. Each summer, the Rainiers offer specialty nights at home games that bring together the local community for fun baseball excitement. Concessions include traditional ballpark favorites and seafood from Ivar's, a local chain famed for their classic fish and chips, fish tacos, chowders, and clams. They even offer the Ivar Dog, a seafood-based hot dog loaded with coleslaw and tartar sauce.

2502 S Tyler St., 253-752-7707
milb.com/tacoma

### TIP

If you arrive early for a game and want to kill some time, walk across the street to the Tacoma Nature Center. Enjoy a hike or let the kids play at the playground.

42

# EXPERIENCE A TRADITIONAL LINKS GOLF COURSE

## AT CHAMBERS BAY

Golf lovers will enjoy playing a few rounds at one of the most stunning courses in the United States. From its humble beginnings as a weed-covered gravel pit, it has become one of the top public golf courses in the nation. Chambers Bay offers one of the few links courses in the United States. Traditionalists love these courses for their resemblance to St Andrews, where golf was founded. You will feel that mystical quality playing the course with its rugged dunes and seaside grasses. The course takes advantage of the natural features of the property to create a special experience. It is rare that you can experience tournament-quality golf on a public course. Chambers Bay was host to the PGA 2015 US Open. The Grill is known for its panoramic views and draws not only golfers but savvy locals as well.

6320 Grandview Dr. W, University Place, 253-460-4653
chambersbaygolf.com

43

# HIKE
## THE TACOMA NARROWS BRIDGE

The Tacoma Narrows Bridge is infamous for its "Galloping Gertie," where old videos show the bridge buckling and swaying before collapsing into the narrows. No worries now. The current bridge is safe and affords magnificent views of the area, including of Mount Rainier from the crest of the bridge. Park at War Memorial Park, which deserves a quick exploration of its military history exhibits. The Narrows Bridge hike follows a 3.4-mile out-and-back paved path. It is considered moderately steep with a consistent 5 percent grade peaking at 8 percent, but the intensity of the hike rewards you with its epic views. Monitor wind conditions, as it can get extremely windy through the narrows and at times it is not safe to hike the bridge.

War Memorial Park
624 N Meyers St.

## TIP

Local legend has it that the King Octopus lives among the ruins of the original Tacoma Narrows Bridge. It is said to weigh 600 pounds and have massive tentacles that can grab those who explore too closely. In reality, octopuses live hiding among the ruins but top out at 50 pounds. You can see the real deal at the Point Defiance Zoo and Aquarium. Many local shops carry books and octopus toys. It is a fun story to share with children.

# EXPLORE THE PUGET SOUND
## WITH DESTINY HARBOR TOURS

Destiny Harbor Tours offers fascinating two-hour boat tours beginning at the marina near the entrance to the Museum of Glass. Guests climb aboard the *Destiny*, named for Tacoma, the "City of Destiny." The trip begins with a tour of the Thea Foss Waterway, where guests will have unique city views of Tacoma, including the famed Stadium High School, two bridges, as well as the grain terminal and two US Navy reserve ships. Tacoma is a busy port, so this trip gives visitors insight into port operations and the opportunity to observe cargo ships, tugs, and barges.

The voyage is very informative about more than just man-made features. Guests can observe seals, bald eagles, and other wildlife. The natural vistas of Mount Rainier and the Olympic Mountains are stunning on a sunny day. The guides are informative and take the time to point out the islands and other waterfront locations. Late in the season, you may even see a pod of orcas as they head into the South Sound following the annual salmon run.

1817 Dock St., 253-225-6306
destinyharbortours.com

## TIP

Tours are seasonal, and even in the summer months it can get quite cold on the water. Dress in layers; a pullover and a light windbreaker are perfect.

# SWIM
## AT AMERICAN LAKE

American Lake Park beckons with its swimming beach located on the north shore of American Lake. The lake has a rich history from the Steilacoom and Nisqually tribes to the wealthy from Tacoma who built lavish estates along the shores of the lake. Fishermen troll along inlets fishing for cutthroat and rainbow trout and a variety of bass stocked by the Washington Department of Fish and Wildlife.

Visitors have access to a beach, a public boat launch, picnic tables, and a playground; during warmer months a vendor rents kayaks. The City of Lakewood authorized multimillion-dollar improvements, which will include an accessible merry-go-round, a new picnic shelter, and other infrastructure improvements scheduled for completion in May 2025.

9222 Veterans Dr. SW, Lakewood, 253-983-7887
cityoflakewood.us/american-lake-park

## TIP

Rent a kayak and paddle along the shoreline to view the historic homes. Back in the day, Tacoma's wealthy built estates next to the lake, including the iconic Thornewood Castle.

46

# OBSERVE WETLANDS
## FROM THE BOARDWALK AT MCKINLEY PARK

Parks Tacoma McKinley Park is one of the oldest parks in Tacoma, established in 1901. It was renamed for President William McKinley after he was assassinated. The park contains important ecosystems due to its four wetlands and streams. These transitional areas between land and sea have rich nutrients the help clean the water before it flows into the Puget Sound.

The park has a nice playground and seasonal restrooms, but the crown jewel of the park is the trails, which take walkers across a boardwalk, around the wetlands, and through lush woods. A distinctive historical feature is a concrete wall that formed a pool with water from a natural spring. In the 1900s, children would swim and cool off on hot summer days. While on the trails, keep an eye out for art made from nature and the interpretive signs that give a glimpse into the history of the area. Birding is also a popular activity due to the wetlands.

907 Upper Park Dr., 253-305-1000
parkstacoma.gov/place/mckinley-park

# HIKE
## THE SEQUALITCHEW CREEK TRAIL

This is the trail locals hike, some every day. It is just stunning from beginning to end. Park at Dupont City Hall, which has the only available restrooms during the trek. It begins by the interpretive signs. Once you start you are quickly enveloped in a magical forest of Douglas firs, rich green mosses, and ferns. The old railroad bed takes you 1.5 miles along a ravine, gradually dropping down to the Puget Sound and a rocky beach. Toward the end you'll see interpretive signs next to the saltwater marsh before crossing under a railroad by tunnel. Trains run frequently, and children love to stand in the tunnel as trains roar above. From the beach you will have views of the Puget Sound islands and the Olympic Mountains in the distance. Harbor porpoises and seals are often spotted from this area. The trip back is uphill, but it is a gentle slope and not too strenuous. The trail is well maintained and stroller friendly until you get to the beach, where it is very rocky.

1700 Civic Dr., DuPont
wta.org/go-hiking/hikes/dupont-sequalitchew-creek

# DISCOVER THE OUTDOORS
## IN AN URBAN NATURE PRESERVE AT THE TACOMA NATURE CENTER

The Tacoma Nature Center is a fun, free activity families will love. Explore the more than two miles of walking trails that meander through a forest and wetlands. Deer are often spotted as well as a variety of bird species. The flat, even trail is very stroller friendly. It is hard to believe you are in the middle of town and not on an epic hike when on the trails. Discovery Pond is a fun play area for children that is not your average playground. Exploring and creative play is encouraged with a boulder scramble, a snag climb, a pond with waterfalls, a log crossing, a tree house, and so much more you'll have a hard time getting the kids to leave. Indoors you will find the Interpretive Center, which has interactive exhibits on wetlands, the watershed, and wildlife. The gift shop offers nature-themed gifts, toys, and tools for nature exploration.

1919 S Tyler St., 253-404-3930
tacomaparks.com
parkstacoma.gov/place/tacoma-nature-center

# HOPE FOR THE ENVIRONMENT AT DUNE PENINSULA PARK

Dune Peninsula is built on what was once part of the Asarco smelter site, one of the first Superfund sites and one of the most polluted areas in the country. Today the Point Defiance and Point Ruston waterfront is one of the most beautiful in the nation and a true environmental success story. Dune Peninsula is named after the book *Dune*, by native son Frank Herbert, whose plot includes a group trying to restore a planet's environment. The winding paved pedestrian loop through the peninsula was named the Frank Herbert Trail. The 11-acre park is landscaped with native drought-tolerant plants and has quickly become a popular place for walks or for just contemplating the gorgeous views of the Puget Sound, local islands, Mount Rainier, and the Port of Tacoma. The Wilson Way Bridge connects Point Ruston and Point Defiance and has an overlook named "the Moment" to encourage taking some time to appreciate the beauty around you. There are six slides next to the bridge that will take you down to the marina below. Or use the adjacent steps. It has been nicknamed "Chutes and Ladders."

5361 Yacht Club Rd., 253-305-1090
parkstacoma.gov/place/dune-peninsula

# LEARN THE HISTORY
## OF INDIGENOUS PEOPLE ON THE PUYALLUP TRIBE WALK

This is a digital guided tour that is just fascinating. Download the GeoTourist app to access the tour and start in Tollefson Plaza. Your guide is Charlotte Basch, a tribal member and the historic education coordinator for the Puyallup Tribe of Indians. She will take you on a two-mile walk beginning in Tollefson Plaza and moving through downtown, sharing the history of the Puyallup and their interactions with the land and the city as you go. Tacoma was once the site of a major Puyallup village, which Basch describes via reference to the tribe's oral history and recent archaeological evidence. There are seven stops along the way, and at each one Basch shares its significance to the Puyallup. The tour takes you along the Prairie Line Trail, which was once part of the Northern Pacific Railroad. It contains artwork and interpretive signs throughout.

17th St. and Pacific Ave.
geotourist.com/tours/4119

### TIP

During or after taking the Puyallup Tribal Walk, enjoy a locally produced beer at 7 Seas Brewing Co., which borders the trail. It is a historic building and was formally the site of the Heidelburg Brewing Co., an iconic Tacoma brewer.

# LEARN GARDENING
## AT SEHMEL HOMESTEAD PARK

Sehmel Homestead Park, as its name suggests, was the Sehmel family's farm where they homesteaded for over 110 years. The site is now a beautiful park that has modern amenities for recreation. Visitors can enjoy tennis courts, a basketball court, baseball, softball, and soccer fields as well as a Boundless Playground (accessible for all abilities). A popular family activity is to meander along the four miles of trails through a forest, wetlands, and a meadow.

Gardeners will love the Heritage Garden and the Washington State University Demonstration Garden. During the spring and summer, learn from master gardeners as they host Saturday Garden Talks. Children love the Youth Program Workshops. The courses are varied, from general ones like "Get Your Garden Growing" or "Reimagining Your Lawn" to specific ones like "Confessions of a Begonia Addict" or "Growing Tomatoes in the PNW." The garden is open year-round.

10123 78th Ave. NW, Gig Harbor, 253-858-3400
penmetparks.org/parks/sehmel-homestead-park

# EXPLORE THE BEAUTY
## OF CHAMBERS CREEK REGIONAL PARK

This beautiful waterfront park has it all. Saltwater shoreline, urban creek and canyon, and epic views of mountains and the Puget Sound all vie for your attention. It wasn't always so lovely. The 930-acre park was once a sand and gravel mine. Legacy structures form iconic backdrops to the natural surroundings. The highlight of the park is its many trails, most of which are paved. Park at the bottom and take the Loop Trail, which combines the Grandview and the Soundview trails. You want to do the strenuous hike up the trail to the bluff first. It is not too bad after that, as you walk along the bluff, down a hill at the other end, and then loop back to the parking lot. There is a bridge that crosses over the railroad tracks to the beach. From it you can see Ketron, Anderson, McNeil, and Fox Islands. Keep an eye out for orcas, which occasionally visit this area. On a nice day, the beach is pleasant to stroll.

6320 Grandview Dr. W, University Place, 253-798-4141
piercecountywa.gov/1317/chambers-creek-regional-park
chamberscreekfoundation.org/trails

# LEARN TO BOULDER
## AT CLIMB TACOMA

Bouldering is a subset of rock climbing that does not require any special equipment beyond a pair of climbing shoes. It is not for the faint of heart as climbers attempt 12-to-18-foot walls with no safety equipment. When a climber inevitably falls, it is onto a padded surface. The sport has so many mental and physical benefits: A bouldering route is a problem that must be solved, and it requires strength, agility, and technique. Benefits include building lean muscle and core strength, improving cardiovascular health, and improving flexibility.

Climb Tacoma has a huge facility that includes 4,500 square feet of bouldering. Wall angles vary from 10 to 70 degrees, and new routes are set each week. Other features include a moon board, a spray wall, a campus board, and a kids' wall. Weights and cardio equipment are available in the fitness area. Surprisingly, if you have a well-behaved pet, they can join you at Climb Tacoma.

3729 S Lawrence St., 253-683-4791
climbtacoma.com

# GO SEE SOME SNOW
## AT CRYSTAL MOUNTAIN RESORT

We have a saying, "Live like the Mountain is Out," based on the idea that if you can see Mount Rainier, then it is a gorgeous day to get outside. Crystal Mountain Resort offers fun outdoor activities both summer and winter. Take a ride on the Mount Rainier Gondola up 2,400 vertical feet to experience breathtaking views of Mount Rainier and more-distant mountains of the Cascades. Even during summer months there is snow on the mountain. In warmer months, discover the natural beauty of the Cascade Range by hiking the ridgelines and witnessing nature waking up after months of hibernation. In the winter months, hit the slopes. Crystal Mountain offers lessons and rentals with everything you need for a day of skiing or snowboarding. Snowshoeing is a great way to explore the winter scenery on foot with a professional guide. After spending time on the mountain, visit the Summit House, Washington's highest-elevation restaurant. At 6,872 feet, you'll dine with gorgeous views of Mount Rainier. Menu changes seasonally.

33914 Crystal Mountain Blvd., Enumclaw, 833-279-7895
crystalmountainresort.com

## TIP

Mount Rainier National Park has two high elevation areas you can drive to: Paradise, which is open year-round; and Sunrise, which typically opens late June each year. Both have snow well into July. On a hot summer day, a trip up to the park will offer cooler temperatures.

# LEARN ABOUT PACIFIC NORTHWEST ANIMALS
## AT NORTHWEST TREK

Northwest Trek Wildlife Park is not your typical zoo, as it offers many opportunities to get up close with Pacific Northwest animals in their natural habitat. The Free-Roaming Area is home to herds of Roosevelt elk, bison, moose, caribou, bighorn sheep, mountain goats, swan, and deer on 435 acres that includes forest, meadow, and a lake. The park offers a variety of tours to experience this area. Eagle Passage will have visitors marveling at bald eagles in a habitat that includes old-growth Douglas firs. These eagles were injured and can't survive in the wild. If you luck out, you may see a bald eagle in the wild flying around the exhibit with the eagles "talking" to each other. Children will love the Kids' Trek playground with its Pacific Northwest theme. Such a fun unique playground made to resemble the forest. Take a stroll on the Animal Walking Paths to observe grizzlies, cougars, and more. Keep an eye out, as they can be anywhere in their large habitats.

11610 Trek Dr. E, Eatonville, 360-832-6117
nwtrek.org

## TIP

Book an Elk Bugling tour during September. The rut is the elk breeding season, and the males lose their minds. You hear the eerie sounds of their bugling and the loud clash of antlers as they spar for female attention.

# DISCOVER A VARIETY OF ACTIVITIES AT THE SPRINKER RECREATION CENTER

Families can spend a full day at the Sprinker Recreation Center and not run out of things to do. At the NHL regulation ice rink, visitors can try out the Ice Bumper cars or join a free skate session. Both figure skating and hockey lessons are available. The center offers four indoor tennis and five racquetball courts. The center offers a variety of art and crafts classes and seminars throughout the year.

The outdoor amenities are where the center really shines. It has one of the largest outdoor skateboarding parks in Western Washington. Learn how to rock climb on the man-made Spire Rock. It is made from a variety of stone blocks including granite that are cemented together creating different surfaces, cracks, and crevices. At one end of the parking lot, guests can access the hiking trails through the Bresemann Forest for a lovely outdoor experience. In the summer months, pack a picnic and enjoy the playground and seasonal splash park.

521 Military Rd. S., 253-798-4000
piercecountywa.gov/1310/Sprinker-Recreation-Center

# UP YOUR GOLF GAME
## AT EVERGREEN GOLF CLUB

Washington is known for its rain, and although local golfers will play year-round, it is nice to have another option. At Evergreen Golf Club, guests can have a next-level golf experience utilizing the latest innovations in golf technology and training. If you've ever wanted to play one of the world's prestigious golf courses, try one of the club's Trackman Simulator Bays. Play Valderrama or the historic St Andrews. The Putt View Putting Green allows golfers to analyze and track their putts to learn how to read the green. There is also a short game complex, which is like mini golf but designed to improve a golfer's short game.

The club has an extensive selection of training programs and golf instructors to help take your game to the next level. Get fit for golf with fitness and physical therapy by Golfletica. Improve your mental game with mental and life training.

2101 Mildred St. W, Fircrest, 253-323-4653
evergreengolfclub.com

# TAKE A NATURE WALK
## AT FORT STEILACOOM PARK

On lands where the Nisqually and Steilacoom Indian tribes sourced their food and Fort Steilacoom once stood is the beautiful Fort Steilacoom Park. The park is full of amenities including a state-of-the-art baseball stadium. A new display at the park is the Tenzler Log, also known as "The Big One." It is a cross section from one of the largest Douglas fir trees ever cut down. It weighs over nine tons and is 12 feet in diameter.

The Waughop Lake Trail is a nature walk that loops around Waughop Lake. The nearly one-mile trail is paved and flat, making it very accessible for all levels and perfect for strollers and bicycles. Along the way there are Discovery Trail educational signs detailing the history of the area. Nature lovers will enjoy observing birds and other wildlife along the trail and from one of the two docks. Benches are located along the trail for a rest or just to contemplate nature.

8714 87th Ave SW, Lakewood, 253-983-7887
cityoflakewood.us/fort-steilacoom-park

# EXPLORE LAND AND SEA
## AT POINT DEFIANCE ZOO AND AQUARIUM

You really get a lot of bang for your buck at the Point Defiance Zoo and Aquarium, where not only can you experience land animals but also creatures under the sea at the Pacific Seas Aquarium. It is all situated overlooking the Puget Sound. The Pacific Seas Aquarium is the newest feature of the park. One of the most popular features is Baja Bay, which has a unique architectural feature that allows the sharks and marine animals to swim overhead. Although there are plenty of large mammals like the majestic elephants, kids and adults alike are drawn to the Kids Zone to watch the meerkats frolic in their habitat. There is a fun zoo-themed playground, and you can even feed the goats.

5400 N Pearl St., 253-404-3800
pdza.org

60

# BEACHCOMB
## ALONG THE PUGET SOUND

Tacoma is a waterfront city, and there are plenty of parks at which to enjoy a day at the beach. The land Titlow Park and Lodge sits on was used by the Puyallup and Nisqually Indians as a campsite. In its heyday around 1911, the lodge was the Hotel Hesperides, where guests came to enjoy the views of the Olympic Mountains, Fox Island, and the Puget Sound. Today, visitors enjoy the extensive beach frontage and an estuary lagoon, which can be explored on two miles of trails. There are plenty of amenities with a sprayground, playground, picnic areas, and plenty of places for various sports activities. The sandy shoreline is a perfect venue for kayaking or paddleboarding. In the quaint town of Steilacoom, you will find Sunnyside Beach, which is popular with scuba divers and snorkelers because it is away from the strong narrows current and because of the marine life found there. The beachfront park also has a nice playground and plenty of picnic tables.

## TWO LOCAL BEACHES

**Titlow Park & Lodge**

8425 6th Ave., 253-305-1000
metroparkstacoma.org/place/titlow-park-lodge

**Sunnyside Beach**

Chambers Creek Rd., 253-581-1912
townofsteilacoom.org/264/Sunnyside-Beach

W.W. Seymour Conservatory

# CULTURE AND HISTORY

# WONDER AT MOLTEN GLASS
## AT THE MUSEUM OF GLASS

As its name suggests, the Museum of Glass (MOG) is dedicated to showcasing works of art created out of glass. It is a very challenging medium to work with. There are live glass demonstrations each day the museum is open. The Hot Shop Team collaborates with visiting artists to bring to life the creative processes and techniques involved in creating a sculpture from molten glass. Tacoma native Dale Chihuly is known worldwide for his expressive glass art. The *Spotlight on Dale Chihuly* exhibition is in the museum's permanent collection and showcases examples of the various stages of his work. A highlight is the Gibson Chandelier, a visually stunning work of art. Art Deco aficionados will delight in almost 200 pieces of René Lalique's artwork from the Steven and Roslyn Shulman Collection. For a truly unique souvenir, visit the museum shop, where you can purchase a one-of-a-kind item designed and created in the MOG's Hot Shop and signed by the team.

1801 Dock St., 253-284-4750
museumofglass.org

# MAKE SOME ART
## AT THE TACOMA ART MUSEUM

The Tacoma Art Museum (TAM) focuses on the art and artists of the Northwest. The permanent collection of over 5,000 artworks includes works by Tacoma native Dale Chihuly. Families will enjoy the TAM Studio in the museum's lobby. No museum admission required. Inspired by the works of art in the TAM's collection, the hands-on activities are sure to inspire your budding artists. The studio is stocked with art supplies and lots of fun things to do. Check out the current "Invitation to Create," which includes ideas and the materials needed to create a project. Readers will love the complete collection of Caldecott Medal–winning picture books to be enjoyed in the Betty Gene and John Walker Reading Alcove.

1701 Pacific Ave., 253-272-4258
tacomaartmuseum.org

## 63

# DISCOVER CHIHULY
## AT UNION STATION

A stop at Union Station is a must when visiting downtown Tacoma. Superstar famed glass artist Dale Chihuly was born and raised in the gritty city. He has generously donated public works of art to various venues around town. His works shown at Union Station were created specifically for the site and beautifully enhance the historic train station. Built in 1911, the domed Union Station was designed by Reed & Stem, the architects acclaimed for New York's Grand Central Station. The Romanesque Revival style of the building makes the perfect backdrop for Chihuly's work. One of his signature chandeliers hangs in the rotunda and is stunning. Although you can see all the works from the first floor, take a moment to walk upstairs and observe them up close. Best of all, the entire experience is free and conveniently located next to the Tacoma Art Museum and the Washington State History Museum.

1717 Pacific Ave., 253-863-5173
travelTacoma.com/listings/union-station/198

64

# PLAY AT THE CHILDREN'S MUSEUM OF TACOMA

The Children's Museum of Tacoma is geared toward children ages birth to 12 with a "Pay as You Will" policy that makes access available to all families regardless of income. There are five nature-inspired play areas, which support unstructured play. Budding artists can hone their skills in the art studio while the little library of children's books inspires a love of reading. The museum has low-sensory hours for those with autism and other sensory sensitivities.

The museum offers Wee Ones Weekly, known as WOW, which is a thematic musical program for toddlers and preschoolers. Play to Learn is a free program held throughout Pierce County. It is a structured program for children under 6 and adults who nurture them. Enjoy individual play time, group activities, songs, and so much more. The curriculum stresses the importance of play in childhood development.

1501 Pacific Ave., 253-627-6031
greentrike.org/childrens-museum-of-tacoma

# GET AWESTRUCK
## ON THE CHIHULY BRIDGE OF GLASS

The Chihuly Bridge of Glass is a stunning public work of art that consists of three distinct installations—the Seaform Pavilion, the Crystal Towers, and the Venetian Wall—created by Tacoma native Dale Chihuly. It is a pedestrian bridge that links the Foss Waterway and the Museum of Glass to Tacoma. From the Museum of Glass, you will come to the Venetian Wall, which displays 109 glass sculptures by Chihuly. The 80-foot-long wall contains some of the largest glass pieces ever blown. Next up are the Crystal Towers, which are massive translucent blue structures created from glass. The inspiration was the glacial, blue ice found at Mount Rainier. These make for an iconic Tacoma image that appears different in the changing light. They form a beacon when illuminated at night. The Seaform Pavilion is so named due to the more than 2,000 objects in its ceiling that create the illusion of being underwater. The Museum of Glass offers a walking tour of the Bridge of Glass and the Thea Foss Waterway.

museumofglass.org/visit

# REFLECT ON MISTAKES OF THE PAST
## AT THE TACOMA CHINESE RECONCILIATION PARK

This lovely park serves as a reminder of the shameful past when a large group of men physically expelled the Chinese people from Tacoma. In the days that followed, townspeople destroyed their homes and businesses. Located on Ruston Way, the park is intended as a place of healing and harmony, and you do have a sense of peace as you walk through this tranquil garden located near the site of the early Chinese settlement called Little Canton. To explore the park, begin at the entrance by the large sign and read about this history. Then follow the interpretive path through the Chinese garden while taking in the natural beauty of Commencement Bay. There are a variety of exhibits and artworks along the way. The park is part of the Ruston Way Waterfront, which is a series of parks connected by a paved path. There is public parking all along the way. Arrive early, as it is very popular.

1741 N Schuster Pkwy., 253-330-8828
tacomachinesepark.org

# EXPLORE
## THE OLD CITY HALL HISTORIC DISTRICT

The Old City Hall Historic District is filled with buildings from the late 1880s to the early 1900s. There was a surge of building during this period as Tacoma became the western terminus of the Northern Pacific Railroad's Transcontinental line. As a result, Tacoma became known as the "City of Destiny," and this was the city's first big building boom. As you walk through this historic district, you will see buildings that were designed by some of the top architects in the Pacific Northwest.

Old City Hall was completed in 1893 in the Italianate style, and its iconic clock tower has long been a Tacoma landmark. It is currently undergoing extensive renovations and will soon be filled with residences, restaurants, shops, and small businesses. Across the street is the Northern Pacific building, also constructed in the Italianate style. Not far away is Fireman's Park, the site of the first fire station. Its signature feature is a totem pole carved by native Alaskans in 1903.

625 Commerce St.
info@oldcityhalltacoma.com

## TIP

Go to the city's website and print off a Walking Tour of the Old City Hall Historic District. You'll also find walking tours of other historic districts in the city.

68

# JUMP BACK IN TIME

## AT THE FORT NISQUALLY LIVING HISTORY MUSEUM

If you ever wanted to know what it was like to reside near the Puget Sound in 1855, then visit the Fort Nisqually Living History Museum located in Point Defiance. This is a 1930s reconstruction of the original fort, which was in Dupont and was the first European settlement on the Puget Sound, built by the Hudson's Bay Company. Volunteers and staff dress in period clothing and demonstrate the work, crafts, and social practices of the times. There are seven buildings. Two of the structures, the Factor's House and Granary, are historical structures preserved and donated by local citizens. All the buildings are historically furnished. The Heritage Gardens offer a unique insight into the history of the fort and reflect 19th-century agricultural practices. Great effort goes into this, including the discovery at a seed bank of a type of wheat grown by the Hudson's Bay Company. There are apple trees grafted from the trees at the original Fort Nisqually site.

5519 Five Mile Dr., 253-404-3970
parkstacoma.gov/exhibits-at-fort-nisqually

## TIP

Hike the Sequalitchew Creek Trail in Dupont, which will give you a feel for the original site of Fort Nisqually.

# LEARN ABOUT MILITARY HISTORY
## AT THE LEWIS ARMY MUSEUM

When driving south on I-5, you can't help but notice the striking white building just past Exit 120. This is the Lewis Army Museum, one of the few buildings on the base dating back to World War I. It is also the only building from Greene Park, which was a recreational area for soldiers stationed at what was then Camp Lewis. It was constructed for the Salvation Army as a Red Shield Inn and in later years became a hotel for soldiers and their families before becoming the Lewis Army Museum. The museum has state-of-the-art exhibits that trace the military history of the base and the units stationed here to the present day. Keep an eye out among the exhibits for a female Asian American soldier with the name Flint, the adopted daughter of the museum director, Erik Flint. There is also a great gift shop with military-themed items and toys for children.

Joint Base Lewis–McChord
4320 Main St. and Constitution Dr.
253-967-7206
lewisarmymuseum.com

## TIP

At Milepost 120 off I-5, stop to see the Captain Meriwether Lewis Monument, the namesake of Fort Lewis and commander of the Corps of Discovery. Also at this site is the iconic Liberty Gate, which was built and paid for by workers who constructed the original Camp Lewis.

# IMMERSE YOURSELF IN MARITIME HISTORY
## AT THE FOSS WATERWAY SEAPORT

This heritage museum is a hands-on way to explore the rich maritime history of Tacoma and the Puget Sound. The museum building is the last remaining section of what was once the longest wheat warehouse in the world. It has been restored and serves as a museum, a boat shop, and an education facility. It even has dock moorage. The Rails Met Sails exhibit brings to life the history of the western terminus for the Northern Pacific Railroad. The scale model of the Tacoma Wharf with running trains is fascinating. Located on traditional Puyallup land, this exhibit seeks to share the rich culture and heritage of the Puyallup people. The active heritage wooden boat shop works to preserve the techniques and craftsmanship of regional boat builders. Make sure to take some time and explore the dock area and the great views of the area.

705 Dock St., 253-272-2750
fosswaterwayseaport.org

**TIP**

Rent a kayak at Foss Harbor Marina and explore the city by water. There are great views of iconic city buildings.

71

# VISIT GRIOT'S GARAGE

Car aficionados need to visit Griot's Garage and Flagship Retail Store housed in a former Coca-Cola bottling facility. From his early years, founder Richard Griot loved to work on cars and care for them. He developed his own line of car-care products to ensure they were made with quality. A visit to the flagship store is a must to tour their museum-quality auto display. Each month the company hosts Caffeine & Gasoline cruise-in car shows, and the cars in the display match the monthly theme. Also, cars used for their catalog covers can often be found in the display. Every time you visit there will be something new.

Take advantage of the free Car Care School. Professionals will demonstrate various techniques for caring for your car including interior detailing, wheels and tires, paint care, and much more. They will show you how to achieve professional results.

3333 S 38th St., 800-345-5789
griotsgarage.com

72

# WALK THROUGH TIME
## AT THE WASHINGTON STATE HISTORY MUSEUM

This huge museum is filled with so many fascinating interactive exhibits that children of all ages will enjoy. *The Great Hall of Washington History—A Window to the Past* is the largest exhibit in the museum. Learn about ancient peoples and Native cultures as well as the early settlers. The large dioramas and hands-on activities will keep your group busy for at least two hours. Make sure to check out the two new galleries that opened in 2021. *Remembrance: The Legacy of Executive Order 9066 in Washington State* is an exhibit about the Japanese American internment during World War II, which began not far from Tacoma on Bainbridge Island. The other new exhibit is *360*, which refers to the 360-mile expanse of the state that runs from the sea to across the Cascades. This unique geography has abundant resources that attracted peoples to establish communities. Check out Anthem Coffee in the museum for a cup of joe or sandwiches.

1911 Pacific Ave., 253-272-3500
washingtonhistory.org

## TIP

The Washington State History Museum is in the Tacoma Museum District. Plan to spend time in the area exploring museums. The Chihuly Bridge of Glass is just a short walk from the museum.

# BECOME AN HONORARY LIGHTKEEPER

## AT BROWNS POINT LIGHTHOUSE PARK

This darling park has a small, recently restored lighthouse and a 1903 historic lighthouse keeper's cottage that you can rent. The accommodations require a "tour of duty," where you raise and lower the flag and log in the weather and shipping traffic. Saturdays add the additional duties of opening the Cottage and Museum for visitors. What a fun experience for families. It is located at the tip of historic Browns Point on the shores of the Puget Sound. Enjoy walking the beach, fishing, and taking in the epic sunsets. The park has plenty of green space and is a perfect site for day visitors to enjoy a picnic. Visitors enjoy watching ships enter the Port of Tacoma or sailboats on nice days. To get here, you drive through the Browns Point Neighborhood with its beautiful old homes. This park is tucked away but well worth the effort to find.

201 Tulalip St. NE, 253-927-2536
pointsnortheast.org

# VISIT THE TACOMA HISTORICAL SOCIETY AND MUSEUM

History comes alive at the Tacoma Historical Society and Museum. Members of the society are passionate about history and want to share it with visitors to their small museum. The historical society strives to make history alive and accessible throughout the year with events like the annual Historic Homes of Tacoma Tour held in May and two events in War Memorial Park.

Check out the museum's rotating exhibits to dive into Tacoma's history and get to know the people and stories behind the City of Destiny. The museum is always free due to generous member support and grants. A recent exhibit, *Bustles to Blue Jeans: 120 Years of Clothing Tacoma*, focused on a century of Tacoma fashion and the evolution of shopping. Purchases at the museum store support the historical society's mission. In addition to Tacoma history books, the shop stocks a wide variety of Tacoma souvenirs such as T-shirts, mugs, jewelry, and seasonal items.

406 Tacoma Ave. S, 253-472-3738
tacomahistory.org

75

# DISCOVER ART AND NATURE
## AT LAKEWOLD GARDENS

Exploring beautiful Lakewold Gardens is a peaceful way to spend an afternoon. The garden has seven formal and natural spaces to explore surrounding the main house. In addition, within these gardens, you will find a plant collection that includes 800 rhododendrons and 30 maples. There are also eight Champion Trees of Washington that represent the largest of a species. After strolling the gardens, explore the mansion and visit the Carroll O'Rourke Library. The Shop at Lakewold Gardens is now located in the house and is filled with a variety of items from local artists and small businesses.

The mission of Lakewold Gardens is to provide intentional encounters with the life-changing power of nature, fostering peace, creativity, and healing in our communities. It's a lofty task but one the foundation succeeds at. There are a variety of art and garden programs offered throughout the year including "Crafting from the Garden," where art is created from nature.

12317 Gravelly Lake Dr. SW, Lakewood, 253-584-4106
lakewoldgardens.org

# EXPLORE
## OLD TOWN TACOMA

The Old Town Business District is known as the birthplace of Tacoma, and the heart is Old Town Park. A replica of founding father Job Carr's log cabin serves as a museum and visitors center in the 1.34-acre park, which also has a playground and paved walking trail. Grab a copy of the walking tour map. When exploring Old Town, watch for commemorative plaques in the sidewalks on North 30th Street that share the stories of famous Tacoma women.

Not far from the park is Old St. Peter's Church, built in 1873, which is the oldest building in Tacoma. Old Town also has some old businesses. Stop at the Spar for lunch or to grab a beer. It is the oldest saloon in Tacoma. Old Town attracted Slavonian and Scadinavian immigrants due to its proximity to the water. Northern Fish Company Old Town was established in 1912 and runs a waterfront market. It is known for its halibut fish and chips.

2350 N 30th St.
info@oldtacomabusiness.org

# LEARN THE LEGEND OF GALLOPING GERTIE

## AT THE HARBOR HISTORY MUSEUM

There is a lot of museum packed in this small place, but every inch is used wisely. The main gallery is stuffed with exhibits on the rich heritage of the Gig Harbor Peninsula. Many are interactive with videos, hands-on displays, or computer exhibits that visitors of all ages will enjoy. The Tacoma Narrows Bridge, which you crossed to get to Gig Harbor, has an infamous past as "Galloping Gertie." The original bridge collapsed in 1940 after buckling and galloping in the high winds. Remnants of the bridge became a reef. Legend has it a giant octopus lives there. Harbor History Museum has an interesting exhibit devoted to Gertie, and you can see video footage of the bridge before it collapsed. During your visit, make sure to go outside to see the restored Midway Schoolhouse and the museum galleries. Experience school at the turn of the century. The *Shenandoah*, a 65-foot purse seiner, was built in 1925 and donated to the museum. It is currently being restored, and you can talk to the volunteers about the process.

4121 Harborview Dr., Gig Harbor, 253-858-6722
harborhistorymuseum.org

78

# IMMERSE IN AUTO HISTORY

## AT LEMAY - AMERICA'S CAR MUSEUM

The stunning, sleek, modern building that houses Lemay - America's Car Museum is an iconic Tacoma landmark and just as impressive as the cars inside. This premier destination for car enthusiasts makes a home for more than 300 automobiles. The museum showcases luxury classics, muscle cars, and rare vintage cars including those from renowned collector Harold Lemay, the museum's namesake. The *Rare & Luxurious* exhibit highlights the history of exceptional and expensive automobiles. Currently on exhibit are a Duesenberg Model J, a Mercedes-Benz 300SL, and many more from auto manufacturers Packard, Cadillac, Ferrari, Shelby, Maserati, and many others. Popular events take place throughout the year including vintage car rallies, film screenings, and auto clubs. The Family Zone offers fun activities for children and adults alike. Make sure to have your photo taken in a 1923 Buick touring car. The souvenir photograph is complimentary. Dine at the Full Throttle Cafe with its eclectic menu.

2702 E D St., 253-779-8490
americascarmuseum.org

# BE ENTHRALLED
## WITH THE RARE PLANTS AT THE W.W. SEYMOUR BOTANICAL CONSERVATORY

Located in Wright Park, a 27-acre arboretum and public park, the W.W. Seymour Botanical Conservatory is a Tacoma treasure. It is one of only three public Victorian-style conservatories on the West Coast and is on the National Register of Historic Places. It opened in 1908 through a generous gift from its namesake. For more than 100 years it has enthralled city residents with its tropical, rare, and exotic plants. In an area where the weather is gray and damp during the winter months, the conservatory provided a warm and beautiful venue with bright colors to dispel the winter blues. The current collection contains ferns, palms, figs, bromeliads, orchids, and many other rare plants. Throughout the year there are floral exhibits and other events. The conservatory gift shop sells plants and other garden-themed merchandise and jewelry. After touring the conservatory, spend some time walking through Wright Park and its more than 700 mature trees.

316 S G St., 253-404-3975
metroparkstacoma.org/place/w-w-seymour-conservatory

80

# VISIT THE STEILACOOM HISTORICAL MUSEUM

Lovely Steilacoom is a city of firsts. It is the first incorporated town in Washington, had the first school district, the first library, the first jail, the first post office, among many more firsts. The main museum building is tiny but packs quite a bit of history in the small space, with so many interesting exhibits. The museum complex also includes two historical buildings, the Nathaniel Orr Home and Orchard, built in 1852, and the Wagon Shop, built in 1870. Volunteer docents are available to answer any questions. The museum has limited hours, but you can still view the sites on a historic walking tour that you can download from the historical society website. The Bair Bistro leases the Bair Drug and Hardware Store, which belongs to the historical society. Step back in time as you enter this living history museum with the walls and shelves lined with relics and photos. Grab a table, order a soda from the original 1908 soda fountain, and enjoy fresh, made-to-order entrées.

1801 Rainier St., Steilacoom, 253-584-4133
steilacoomhistorical.org/steilacoom-walking-tour

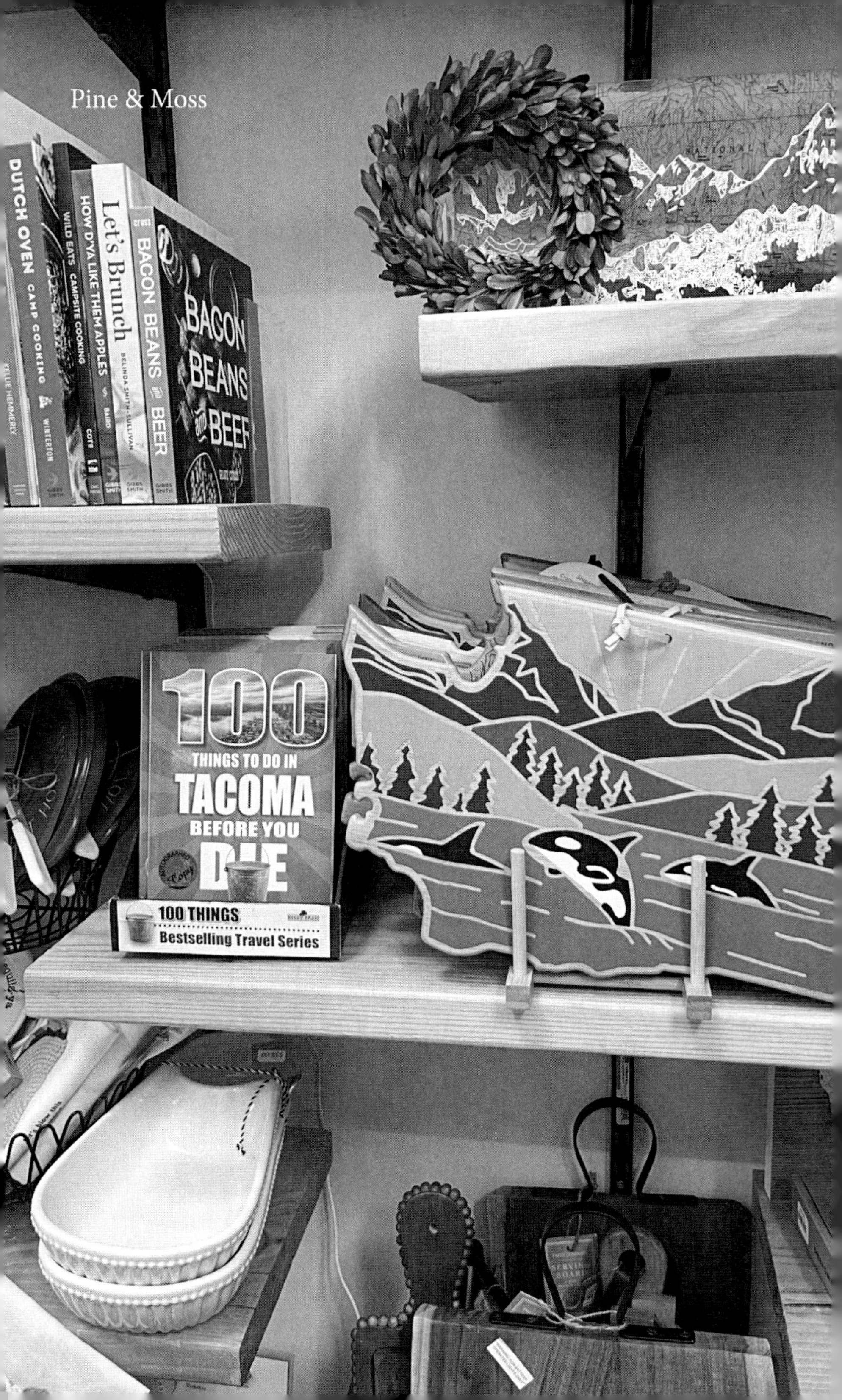
DUTCH OVEN CAMP COOKING
KELLIE HEMMERLY
WINTERTON
WILD EATS CAMPSITE COOKING
COTE
HOW D'YA LIKE THEM APPLES
BAIRD
Let's Brunch
BELINDA SMITH-SULLIVAN
BACON BEANS and BEER
BACON BEANS and BEEF
100 THINGS TO DO IN TACOMA BEFORE YOU DIE
100 THINGS
Bestselling Travel Series
Pine & Moss

# SHOPPING AND FASHION

81

# SHOP TILL YOU DROP
## AT PINE & MOSS

This darling shop is a dream come true for owner Kimberlee Cavin, a retired military spouse. It is not only a store but a community. Kimberlee knows the challenges military spouses face in finding employment, so she tries to hire them. She also sources locally as much as possible from artists and purveyors around the Pacific Northwest. Pine & Moss is a go-to shop for gifts, and with local food artisans (products so good they should be called art) like Seattle Chocolates and Coro Foods (handcrafted charcuterie) you can find gourmet additions to up your picnic game. There is an eclectic mix of children's toys, clothing, skin care products, and home decor. There truly is something for everyone. Cavin combines her southern heritage with the Pacific Northwest spirit to create a unique shop inspired by tradition with a modern flair.

1408 Palisade Blvd., DuPont, 253-355-6879
shoppineandmoss.com

82

# SHOP AND EAT
## AT MARLENE'S NATURAL FOODS & DELI

Marlene's Natural Foods & Deli is a one-stop shop for everything organic, green, and sustainably produced. This family-owned-and-operated natural food store has strict standards for everything they offer for sale. A visit here includes grocery shopping, exploring what's new in the mercantile, and then enjoying a healthy lunch at the deli. With so many choices for lunch it is hard to choose from the fresh, house-made soups, entrées, sandwiches, smoothies, and the bakery.

The produce department is stocked with 100 percent organically grown fruits and vegetables, which come from local farms as much as possible. Marlene's sources from international farms that adhere to their strict rules for healthy working environments, organic growing practices, and fair wages. The mercantile has beautiful items from local artisans as well as a variety of fair-trade goods from around the world. The selection includes candles, wind chimes, organic clothing, jewelry, and much more. It is a perfect spot to shop for gifts.

2951 S 38th St., 253-472-4080
marlenesmarket-deli.com

83

# EXPLORE KOREAN SHOPPING
## AT SHIN SHIN

Shin Shin is a Korean home goods store filled with all kinds of unique treasures. Korean skin care has seen a surge in popularity, especially the paper face masks, which are a steal here. Children will love the training chopsticks. Although Shin Shin primarily features home goods, make sure to go down every aisle, as you never know what you will find. There are lots of Korean herbal remedies, like ginseng. Also take time to watch the videos demonstrating Korean kitchen appliances. So interesting. Be prepared for excellent customer service, which can be a little intimidating if you aren't used to the culture. The salespeople are not following you because they think you are stealing but to help you with your selections and to make suggestions. Truly a fun adventure and a cultural experience.

8726 S Tacoma Way, 253-582-2975
facebook.com/shin-shin-185403424809526

84

# WANDER
## WATSON'S GREENHOUSE AND NURSERY

Visiting a greenhouse and nursery in a travel guide? Absolutely! In addition to gardening, Watson's has a 32,500-square-foot glass-and-steel greenhouse from Belgium that is stunning. Shop the extended line of gifts and garden art as well as gardening products and plants. Watson's grows most of their annuals and makes their own containers and hanging planters. Take the time to walk the rows and view all the beautiful plants, especially in spring and summer. The designers are pros and they put together some gorgeous containers with unique plant combinations. Perfect for a hostess gift when visiting friends or family. After you work up an appetite, visit the on-site Fran's Garden Bistro. With its cute "ladies who lunch" vibe, it is a fun place to eat. The menu offers paninis, sandwiches, soups, salads, and quiche. The soups are house-made daily, and the bistro offers daily specials.

6211 Pioneer Way E, Puyallup, 253-845-7359
shop.watsonsgreenhouse.com

# DON'T GET LOST
## AT FREIGHTHOUSE SQUARE

What an eclectic experience it is exploring Freighthouse Square! This plucky group of entrepreneurs runs a variety of businesses, many of them minority owned, in an iconic historic building that continues to reinvent itself. Built around 1910, it was once the Milwaukee–St. Paul Railroad Station and Freighthouse and now has a faded vintage feel to it that is part of its charm. The businesses come and go, so you never know what you will find, but it is sure to be interesting. The building is huge, spanning three blocks at five stories tall. It houses everything from antique shops, art galleries, kitschy shops, and even an escape room. The food court has a local cult following, and you will find an international mix of food choices there. Make sure to visit the Olive Branch Café, which is decorated with reclaimed items. It is beautifully historic looking and offers lunch and tea. Free parking is available across the street in the parking garage. It is at the Tacoma Dome Station, where you can catch the Link light-rail, which will take you downtown.

2501 E D St., 253-305-0678
visitpiercecounty.com/listing/freighthouse-square/96

## TIP

On the corner opposite Freighthouse Square you will see a warehouse building and a yellow door, the entrance to Johnny's Fine Foods. This iconic local brand has been around for over 70 years, and the seasoning salt of choice for area chefs is Johnny's. It is their top-selling product, and while you can find it in local stores, it is a fun experience going through the yellow door, into the office to purchase Johnny's products.

86

# STOCK UP
## AT STOCKLIST GOODS & GIFTS

Owner Liz Van Dyke opened Stocklist Goods & Gifts in 2016 after 15 years of working in retail for other shops. She is a graduate of Tacoma's Spaceworks incubator program, which helps entrepreneurs open a thriving business. In addition to her storefront, she also has successful online sales.

Locals and visitors alike love her shop. Friendly and helpful customer service is the cornerstone of the store's success. Van Dyke has a great eye for what to stock, especially when it comes to local products. She's been known to pass out chocolate to enjoy while shopping. The shop has an eclectic selection including Cavallini & Co. puzzles. They are popular, so she added a puzzle hall of fame to her website. For those looking for souvenirs of Tacoma, there is a wide variety of options. Choose from colorful coasters, refrigerator magnets, T-shirts, vintage postcards, and very unique glassware that is handblown with local mountains molded into the base.

1934 Pacific Ave., 253-720-0062
stocklistgoods.com

# VISIT UPTOWN GIG HARBOR

## FOR UPSCALE SHOPPING

This is upscale-boutique shopping at its finest. Vibrant Uptown Gig Harbor's mission is to make shopping fun again, and they do, with an outdoor shopping center designed like a town plaza. The vibe here is relaxed and friendly. Grab a cup of coffee and stroll the Art Walk that takes you through the landscaped grounds where you can experience all types of art from contemporary sculpture to traditional gongs. Shoppers will love the 35 chic retailers that are a mix of national chains and local merchants. For entertainment, enjoy one of the many restaurants from quick takeout to fine dining. Watch a movie at the Galaxy Theater and IMAX. Before visiting, make sure to view the website for fun events such as performances by local school bands or individual store events like "sip and shop." Also look for specials. There is always something on sale.

4701 Point Fosdick Dr., Gig Harbor, 253-851-4557
uptowngigharbor.com

# CRAFT A MASTERPIECE
## AT TINKERTOPIA

Children and adults love coming in to Tinkertopia, where their imaginations can run wild. Founded by two Tacoma artists, Tinkertopia strives for planetary-resource conservation, more commonly known as “upcycling.” They work with local industries to repurpose scraps, discards, and overstocks into low-cost arts-and-crafts supplies. The bonus is that it helps the environment by removing these items from the waste stream. So many options. You can purchase bags of varying sizes and fill them with what you like from the amazing selection. Out-of-towners often find a unique “historic” souvenir, or you can book a 90-minute Tinker Time session to craft your own masterpiece. For the bargain price of $10 you can access the Tinker Space and all the supplies needed. It is such a fun and creative way to enjoy the Tacoma art scene. It’s a great activity for after a museum visit.

1914 Pacific Ave., 253-778-6539
tinkertopia.com

## TIP

Tinkertopia is within walking distance to the Washington State History Museum. Explore the museum in the morning for inspiration and then shop at Tinkertopia to purchase parts to re-create something from history.

# GIVE BACK
## WITH A PURCHASE AT COMPASS ROSE TACOMA

Compass Rose donates 10 percent of their earnings to local charities that improve our community and international nonprofits working to alleviate poverty. The store, located in the charming, historic Proctor neighborhood, houses a thoughtfully curated collection of Pacific Northwest goods, handcrafted jewelry, paper goods, and home decor. The shop is light and colorful, which is important on gray Pacific Northwest days. The decorated displays are arranged to highlight the lovely offerings, each of which is carefully selected. Local is important, as is sustainability, in determining what is worthy to be in the store. If you need a gift, this is the place to go. When finished shopping, take some time to explore this walkable neighborhood filled with Craftsman-style homes, darling shops, and eclectic restaurants.

3815 N 26th St., 253-759-0077
compassroseshop.com

# KNOW WHERE YOUR PURCHASE COMES FROM

## AT MCCOY KIDS

McCoy Kids is not your average toy store. Owners Evan and Lauren carefully curate every item that fills the shelves of their charming shop. They specialize in unique, small batch products of the utmost quality. The couple take the time to learn how each item is produced and how the materials are used. Sustainability is a core value for the company. They make the effort to recycle and reuse packing materials and purchase sustainable materials. When choosing what to carry at the store, the two use their own experience as parents to find unique items that shoppers never knew they needed. When perusing the shop, visitors will learn who the makers of the products are. It makes a difference when a maker puts so much time and effort into their products. McCoy Kids gives back to the community in various ways including supporting local philanthropist Kwabi Amoah-Forson and his Peace Bus mission.

504 S 11th St., Ste. A, 253-242-6076
shopmccoykids.com

# GET LOST EXPLORING
## AT SANFORD AND SON ANTIQUES

Tacoma's Antique Row is made up of a diverse collection of shops and antique stores located in one of the most historic areas of downtown. The granddaddy of them all is the behemoth Sanford and Son Antiques. The store is so large you can enter on the ground floor on Broadway and exit a few stories up on Commerce Street. There are three floors and 25,000 square feet of antiques, books, oddities, and other treasures. It is the largest singly owned antique shop in the Pacific Northwest. There is even a display with the lid of an Egyptian sarcophagus. The Middle Floor Merchants are 20 shops and services that are individually owned. You'll find thousands of books in the library, which is two-tiered and can be rented for events. Spend some time strolling Broadway and explore some of the other stores in the area. Truly a unique experience.

743 Broadway, 253-272-0334
instagram.com/sanfordandsonantiques

# CURE YOUR SWEET TOOTH
## AT THE BROWN AND HALEY FACTORY STORE

This iconic factory–store combo is a must-stop when visiting Tacoma. You can't tour the over-100-year-old factory, but the outside is pretty cool, with its vintage charm and iconic neon light. In 1962, Brown and Haley purchased the ticket booth from the 1962 World's Fair, held in Seattle. Elvis Presley was in the building during the filming of *It Happened at the World's Fair*, where it was used as a green room for him between scenes. This tiny building is a candy lover's dream, with factory-outlet prices on Almond Roca and all the other Rocas, the company's famed concoction. Mountain Bars are another candy they are famed for. The signature gold-and-pink packaging filled with Almond Roca has been popular since 1923. In the 1990s, Almond Roca became the largest exported gift candy in the United States; it is shipped to 63 countries.

110 E 26th St., 253-620-3067
brown-haley.com

# TREAT YOURSELF
## AT JOHNSON CANDY COMPANY

The Johnson family has handcrafted chocolates since 1925 after surviving the early years of a very competitive market. Candymakers fell by the wayside, including Frank Mars, who later found success with the Mars candy company in Minnesota. The Johnson Candy Company's success is due to great products that are made fresh daily by William Johnson and his father, Ron, who still comes in daily. A top seller is the open-faced caramel with roasted California almonds dipped in milk or dark chocolate. The caramel is rich, buttery, and super soft, just firm enough to hold its shape. This is seriously good candy. The company is in the Hilltop neighborhood in its now-iconic building built in 1949. The Link light rail expansion travels right by the Johnson Candy Company.

924 M.L.K. Jr. Way, 253-272-8504
johnsoncandyco.com

94

# DISCOVER
## PACIFIC NORTHWEST PRODUCTS

The Pacific Northwest Shop is a must-stop for both locals and tourists. Locals love to shop here for unique gifts, while visitors can find the perfect souvenir of their trip. These aren't your made-in-China knickknacks with Tacoma stamped on them but a carefully curated selection of local products from around the Pacific Northwest. How unique is a glass Christmas ornament made from ash created when Mount St. Helens erupted? You'll find a great selection of candies, food products, and Washington wines. Regional artists who craft jewelry, pottery, and other artworks are featured. The store is nestled in the Proctor neighborhood, where you will find a variety of shops and restaurants that are easy to explore on foot. It is a fun neighborhood with a vibrant farmers market on Saturday mornings.

2702 N Proctor St., 253-752-2242
pacificnorthwestshop.com

95

# JOIN ONE OF
## INVITATION BOOKSHOP'S MANY BOOK CLUBS

Owners Jason and Allyson Howard saw an opportunity to open an independent bookstore when the local Waldenbooks closed. It took nine years to make their dream a reality, and the local community benefits from their curated selection. Invitation Bookshop is the independent bookstore for those who love to read. Not sure what your next read should be? Check out the staff picks from booksellers who have access to the latest releases coming into the store. If you can't find what you are looking for in the store, helpful clerks can order it for you.

Join one of their four book clubs that meet once a month and receive a discount on the monthly selection. Allyson moderates the Flagship Book Club, which focuses mostly on literary fiction with many selections coming from underrepresented voices in the publishing world. The shop also stocks a wide range of children's books and offers discounts to teachers and schools. The owners offer fundraising book fairs for local schools.

3119 Judson St., Ste. A, Gig Harbor, 253-432-4566
invitationbookshop.com

## ADDITIONAL INDEPENDENT BOOKSHOPS

**Tacoma Book Center**

324 E 26th St.
253-572-8248

**King's Books**

218 St. Helens Ave.
253-272-8801
kingsbookstore.com

# SIP AND SHOP
## AT TACOMA WINE MERCHANTS

Do you love wine and want to learn more about it? Tacoma Wine Merchants is the place to shop. For over 20 years this family-owned bottle shop and wine bar has helped Tacoma's residents find the perfect bottle of wine. Whether it is for a gift, a special occasion, or a bottle that will stand the test of time in a wine cellar, Tacoma Wine Merchants can help you select it. Come in for a visit to their shop in Old Town Tacoma and peruse both domestic and international wines at all price points.

For those looking to learn more about wine, spend some time at the wine bar sampling a wine flight accompanied by a charcuterie or cheese board. Check the calendar for special events like educational tastings with local winemakers and with importers of wines from around the world. The merchants also offer several reasonably priced wine clubs.

2122 N 30th St., Ste. C, 253-779-8258
tacomawinemerchants.com

# CREATE A UNIQUE LOOK
## AT REBELS & LOVERS

Rebels & Lovers is a boutique clothing store with a mission to inspire the fashionista in you. Their mantra is to "Look Beautiful, Feel Powerful." It captures the belief that when you look your best, you feel your best. Stop into the shop to give your wardrobe a breath of fresh air.

The shop has a wide selection of casual outfits, dresses, business attire, and statement pieces. The staff who work here love fashion and love to make their clients look good. Let them help you create a look that is uniquely you. Once you've found your outfit, make sure to check out all the accessories to add that something extra. Rebels & Lovers is located at Point Ruston, which has a variety of shops and restaurants. So after shopping, plan to have lunch or maybe a spa treatment at Spa Serein.

5064 Main St., 253-212-3616
rebelsnlovers.com

98

# PURCHASE EDUCATIONAL TOYS
## AT TEACHING TOYS AND BOOKS

From its opening in 1981, Teaching Toys and Books was unlike other toy stores. Their mission has been to source quality toys that support the emotional, physical, and intellectual growth of the area's children. This approach affects the company's inventory as they search the world for the best quality toys. The company has strict standards for safety and quality for everything they purchase.

Take advantage of the friendly and knowledgeable staff, who are trained to answer questions about the products they carry. There are so many elements to learning, and toys are classified by categories such as independent, creative, or cooperative play, motor skills, visual learning, language development, and many more. Who knew toys could be so educational? The shop has a great reputation for customer service and offers complimentary gift wrapping and a Teaching Toys punch card for frequent shoppers. There are two locations: one in the Proctor District and one in Gig Harbor.

## LOCATIONS

**Teaching Toys and Books**

2624 N Proctor St., 253-759-9853

**Teaching Toys, Too**

4635 Point Fosdick Dr., #300, Gig Harbor
253-514-6113

teachingtoysandbooks.com

# ELEVATE GIFTING
## WITH PAPER LUXE

Laurie Hicks and her daughter, Jennifer Luna, have a devoted fanbase for their retail stores located in Fircrest and Gig Harbor. Their love of all things paper resulted in the first shop, Paper Luxe stationery and gifts. If you are looking for a thoughtful gift, this is the place to shop. Locally themed items perfect for souvenirs and gifts are in the Pacific Northwest section. For those shopping for children check out the Curious Bear Toy & Book Shop located in the same building. This shop offers a carefully curated selection of quality books, STEM and Montessori toys, and so much more. Two additional stores are located in Gig Harbor as well as their Kindship Studio. This new venue hosts creative workshops, the company's wildly popular warehouse sales, and other events. Available to rent for private events such as birthday parties or baby or bridal showers.

Fircrest
2053 Mildred St. W
253-328-4967

Gig Harbor
4729 Point Fosdick Dr. NW, Ste. 300
253-900-2132

The Kindship Studio
4793 Point Fosdick Dr. NW, #200
Gig Harbor, 253-244-0065
thekindship.com

paper-luxe.com

100

# GET INSPIRED
## AT SAGE INTERIORS

Sage Interiors is not your average furniture store. From the moment you walk into their gallery in the Old Nisqually Power Station, your senses are heightened. The historic building is stunning with huge soaring ceilings, original brickwork, and huge windows throughout the building that allow in natural light.

The gallery inspires creativity with its curated collections of furniture and decor. Natural woods, soothing colors, plush upholstery, and rich fabrics echo throughout the building and create a soothing environment. The furniture is high end and the prices reflect that, but there are also budget-friendly accessories that can add a touch of style without breaking the bank. The company's values are committed to sourcing products that are made from natural and sustainable materials. Signature collections meet the highest standards for eco-craftsmanship. Sage Interiors offers a free design service.

2416 S C St., 833-718-0878
sageinteriors.com

# ACTIVITIES BY SEASON

## WINTER



## SPRING

## SUMMER



## FALL

NetShed No. 9

# SUGGESTED ITINERARIES

## FAMILY FUN



## DISCOVER DALE CHIHULY



## DATE NIGHT

## EXPLORE THE GARDENS



## GET OUTSIDE

Thea Foss Seaport

Point Defiance Zoo

# INDEX

Point Defiance Park